AF390034

BE YOUR OWN PILOT

MANISH KUMAR

Book Name: Be Your Own Pilot

Book Author: Manish Kumar

Category: 1. Inspirational-fiction 2. Self-help 3 Spiritual fulfilment

Cover Design by Gaurav

ISBN: 978-81-959297-6-4

©Decemeber 2023

Published by M K Media
206, Tower 7, Golf Avenue 2, Sec 75, NOIDA 201301

Disclaimer

The book is inspired by a true story. The author has taken creative liberty to interpret and fictionalize the events. Names of people, characters, places, and things are fictitious. Any resemblance to anyone living or dead is purely coincidental and not intentional. The narrative is the author's perception and need not be the perception of any person, institution or organisation.

For Sarah, the daughter
I always wanted to have.

Acknowledgements

The book would not have been possible without John Harricharan's inspiration—the lesson of Professor Peterson. Although I had been thinking about this book for a long time, John's personal story made me begin writing.

After that, Nikhil Kripalani of Writerforce liked my concept and had the courage and conviction to take it up. I thank Sandhya Advani for introducing him to me. My gratitude also to Preeti Verma Lal who, through her letters, had helped me master the finer nuances of the English language and to Sunita Kripalani who edited and perfected the manuscript of this book.

A special word of thanks to all the writers whose works have inspired me and countless others such as John Harricharan, Deepak Chopra, Richard Bach, Robin Sharma, Dr Brian Weiss, and Eckhart Tolle, to name a few. I sincerely believe that we are what we read.

My reverence to my parents who gave me the sanskar to be a loving human being, I hope I never let you down, Papa and Ma.

My fondest love to my son Aabhaas who declared that the book would be a bestseller even before it was complete.

And above all my obeisance to the indomitable human spirit, and to you, dear reader, to your power to dream and the power to make your dreams come true…

Manish Kumar

June, 2010

Contents

Foreword by John Harricharan

I lead a very busy life and generally cannot answer the tens of thousands of emails that come to me every month. Much as I would like to respond, it's almost practically impossible. But I do glance through the names to see if there is someone I know, write a short reply and move on.

And so it was that I came upon a note sent to me by Manish Kumar. I don't quite remember when it started, but I kept seeing his name here and there, sometimes on my Facebook page, other times through something a dear friend, Yasminder Verdi, would mention in an email. And that is how I got to know Manish.

It is not that we had met or had daily conversations. After all, he lives on the other side of the planet from where I am. It's more like his spirit was shining so brightly through his words and across the miles that I had to stop and take note. I am happy, very happy that I did.

Why am I happy about this? Because I was given an opportunity to discover a rare treasure. You see, Manish had written a book, "Be Your Own Pilot." He was kind enough to send me a draft copy to look at. I thought I would just glance through it, but then, as I started reading, I could not put it down.

Manish uses the metaphor of flying to bring us some of the most life-affirming messages possible. In simple language, he leads us into a world where we find the gentle hints of that which we need to know. His chapter, "It's all about balance" as well as his formula for success, which he refers to as "IVR" would help anyone to reach goals that may have seemed unreachable.

And, NO, I will not tell you what "IVR" stands for. You will have to find out for yourself and experience the thrill of discovery, just as I did. You will be happy that you found the formula.

My suggestion is that you get yourself a copy of this book, read and reread it. I think you'll find the answers to problems challenging you for quite a while. And while you are at it, pick up a copy for someone near and dear to you. Share it with those you love. They will be grateful, very grateful.

Thank you, Manish, thank you for sharing your insights with us. Thank you for writing a book that has the potential to change many lives. And thank you for giving me the opportunity to read it. I look forward to reading your future books. I am sure many others will, too.

John Harricharan

June 2010

About John Harricharan

"John Harricharan leads us along the enchanted path of enlightenment with magic, charm, love and compassion."

— Deepak Chopra, International Speaker and Author.

John Harricharan was the author of the bestselling books, "When You Can Walk on Water, Take the Boat," "Under the Tamarind Tree," "Power Pause" and many others.

Introduction

Children have a dream and are always excited about achieving it. As kids, we had our dreams but somehow as we grew older, most of us forgot about the dream. The majority of people have lost their dreams or have lost the courage to pursue them.

Our lives have become mundane, doing routine things day in and day out. We go through the motions of living. In fact, we hardly live. We merely exist. We go through our days as if life is a prison term that must be endured. We wind up counting our days. We put our lives on autopilot and sit back, relinquishing all control.

Life is not meant to be lived that way. Every day is meant to be a celebration. A celebration of being alive. Living our dreams or inching towards them. Wouldn't it be great to spread your wings, get off the autopilot of life and say, "I Have the Controls?"

I wish you the courage and conviction to follow your true beliefs and the power to fulfil your dreams.

Manish Kumar

June 2010

Chapter One

I HAVE THE CONTROLS

I had dreamed of it almost every day as far as I can remember, learning to fly, being in the cockpit, and now that day had dawned. I was sitting in the cockpit of a twin-seater piston engine trainer at the Flying Training School. It was my first sortie. The Instructor was doing the pre-start checks. His fingers moved magically over the switches, the lights glowed and the pumps came on. I heard the sound of the fuel gushing into the parched pipes, the buzz of the generator, the tic-tic-tic of the torch igniters, the sound of the turbine moving and suddenly the engine came to life! The smell of aviation fuel filled the cockpit; for me, that aroma was intoxicating.

The blast of air from the propellers cut the stillness of the thin winter air, everything came alive and the trees bowed in obeisance in preparation for the grand event.

My instructor asked permission to taxi. With a wave of the hand, he signalled the ground crew to remove the chocks from the wheels. The crew gave a thumbs-up sign and saluted. The Instructor saluted back, a brisk top gun salute, I had seen it a thousand times, not only in the movies but also with my eyes both open and shut. On releasing the brakes, the plane lurched forward. Soon, we were on the runway, which for me was an entry into a whole new world, a world of limitlessness, a world without boundaries, a world full of unlimited possibilities.

My mind rushed back to the past. Could it really be happening? For a small-town boy who had never seen a plane on the ground, not even the inside of an airport, sitting in a plane for the first time, especially in the cockpit, felt unreal.

I remembered a childhood incident when a friend of ours from a nearby big town made us believe that he had bought a toy plane that could be flown. I had believed him. I had fallen asleep so many times dreaming of it, flying it, taking-off from the playground, flying over trees. I always used to look for large fields from which I could take off and land. I had made my parents take me to the big town, looking for the plane, and I was dismayed when the shopkeepers gave me that strange look. When I confronted my friend, he owned up that it was just a figment of his imagination. I was heartbroken. But the die was cast, my fate was sealed.

Now all I could think of was how to make it come true. Thank God, I had believed his story. Later, I watched a movie in which the hero was flying a plane. He was flying low, chasing a herd of cattle to impress his fiancée. I lived in his boots for days. Once,

I got an old chair and sat in the shallow waters in the river as he had done in the movie. He had worn knee-boots while I was barefoot.

Today was the result of the dogged and persistent pursuit of that dream. Almost every small boy who sees a plane dreams of becoming a pilot, some chase it and a few manage to achieve that dream.

The instructor taxied the aircraft to the runway, held it on brakes and opened full power. The aircraft seemed like a horse at the beginning of a race, rearing to be unleashed. When the instructor released the brakes, it plunged forward, sinking me, pushing me deep into my seat. As the markers on the runway whizzed past, first slowly and then in a blur, it was as if life had been fast-forwarded, with me as a witness.

Victor, the instructor, raised the nose gently and whispered, "Come on, baby," and we were up in the air. It was common for pilots to address their planes thus. For them, an air craft was a living object, to be treated with love and respect, to be handled lovingly and gently, without being disrespectful.

There is something magical about the moment the aircraft leaves the ground, something akin to a yogi's levitation, and for me, being the first time, it was an euphoric, almost orgasmic, experience.

Victor was a tall man in his early thirties with short, grey hair. He glanced at me with a naughty smile. Winking, he asked, "First time in an aircraft?"

"Yes, Sir, how did you guess?"

"Your grunt during take-off and your ear-to-ear smile now."

As we gained altitude, the world below us looked smaller and smaller, almost meaningless. The blue skies above us seemed to invite us to frolic, like a foster mother saying, "Come, child, play in my lap for some more time before you return to your mother."

Victor levelled the plane at 5,000 feet and demonstrated a few turns. Like a child eagerly waiting for his friend to finish a game so that he could also have a go, I waited for my turn to play with my old, imaginary childhood toy. My fingers were twitching. Victor guessed my impatience and said,

"You have the controls."

I automatically replied, "I have the controls" and grabbed the joystick. I already had my hand on the throttle.

"Just feel it, gentle movements…nothing jerky."

It was then that the power of the four words "I have the controls" dawned on me. It was the moment of truth, the moment I was waiting for all my life from the time I first saw a plane and decided to be a pilot. I was actually handling the controls of a plane in flight! I had the power to take it where I wanted.

"Yes, I have the controls," I murmured.

The words had a powerful impact on me. They touched the core of my being, my very existence, and stirred awake something waiting to be awakened. I felt in control of everything, not only the plane but my life, my destiny. I knew that if I could come so far with just a dream, I could achieve anything. I remembered the words I read somewhere:

"You are not given a dream without the power to achieve it."

How true, I thought. What next, I wondered.

Chapter Two

RELEASE YOUR BRAKES FOR TAKE-OFF

The joyride was over. Victor explained, "Every day we will concentrate on one aspect of flying." He demonstrated a take-off and asked me to do one. I managed and was happy to go up in the air. He took over the controls, giving me a weird look. "Was that a take-off?" he asked sardonically.

Analysing every aspect, he pointed out, "The nose of the aircraft was not pointing towards the centre of the centre-line of the runway because the nose wheel was cocked to one side when you stopped in the beginning. Why did you hesitate to release the brakes after you applied full power? A part of you was still struggling to let go, you know. After you had applied the power, what were you waiting for?

"You had done your checks, taken care of everything, checked all the parameters… Remember, you cannot be checking and rechecking just to be too sure, it is called 'analysis-paralysis,' you wait so long to analyse things that you forget to act. You just have to let go.

"And where were you looking when we started rolling? If you look so close, how you will know where you are going? That is why you kept zigzagging on the runway, wasting a lot of it. You have to get airborne within a stipulated time, you cannot take forever. You moved forward, then stopped, then moved forward, and then again you stopped. What were you afraid of? After you have applied full power, just pick up a point of reference for direction and maintain it. Do not let it get out of your sight. Where will you reach if you don't know where you are going?"

Later, I asked myself. Don't most of us commit the same mistakes in our lives? Our hearts and minds point in different directions. They are rarely aligned with what we truly desire in life. Most of us are in jobs and relationships in which our hearts aren't and we don't even seem to care. Even when we try to break off and start afresh, we are reluctant to lose our inhibitions, let go of our limiting beliefs and shed the shackles that hold us down. We fail to realize and utilize our full potential and instead of focusing on our final destination, our short-sighted vision delays us in getting back to our final track. As a result, we do not see the time markers in life's path. All of this leads to a purposeless, meaningless existence.

Chapter Three

YOUR ATTITUDE DETERMINES YOUR ALTITUDE

We were up in the cockpit once again. I was with Victor, who, I learnt, was called Don by his friends. The name did not suit his easy-going friendly personality, but what's in a name, I thought…

The only Don I knew then was the great cricketing legend—Don Bradman. Was Victor a Master of the game played up in the air? Where the boundaries are limitless, but you respect the limits of the plane and push human limits? Instead of fours and sixes, the Masters make figures of eight in the air with their planes. High up in the air, where one attracts the force of gravity manifold and sometimes even negates it, where records are kept in the logbook, where life is the reward for winning and death the ultimate penalty and the best player is the one who survives till the very end.

"Concentrate on your take-off. Do not commit the same mistakes again," said Victor as we taxied to the runway.

I quickly reviewed the mistakes of the previous day and aligned the aircraft on the centre-line. Before I could open the throttle, Victor said, "Just move ahead a little."

As I released the brakes, the aircraft moved at an angle. "Never be too sure. Roll a little on the centre-line."

I got back on the centre-line, picked up a point to maintain direction, opened the throttle and released the brakes. I was amused at my ability to maintain the direction, but when I saw the end of the runway approaching, Victor yelled, "Raise your attitude!"

Before I knew it, he had taken over the controls. We managed to take off just before the end of the runway.

"What was your attitude during the take-off?" he asked sharply.

I was speechless, I couldn't reply. He explained, "Attitude is the position of the aircraft in relation to the horizon. You can look at the horizon outside; also cross-refer to the artificial horizon inside. After you have applied full power, released your brakes and built the momentum, you have to raise your attitude or you will continue to remain on the ground. Remember, your attitude determines your altitude."

"I'll remember that" I responded.

He continued, "The heights by great men reached and kept were not attained by sudden flight, but they while their companions slept, were toiling upward in the night."

"I know that quote, it was H W Longfellow," I said, stressing the poet's name. Victor himself was a tall guy and he smiled at the pun.

"You have people with you who hit the bar every night and there are others who stay up late nights, preparing for the next day. It's all a matter of attitude. You know, it's so easy to do and think as others, but it requires guts to do the contrary. To walk your own path and to think your own thoughts requires courage. This courage comes from having the right attitude. Often, our attitude is set by others. It should instead be set by our own values and core beliefs. The way you fly tells a lot about your attitude towards life in general and towards yourself in particular. We must check our attitude not only from the worldly horizon but also look inside at our own internal reference system."

Victor was using too many metaphors, but he was right. Our success in life does depend on our attitude. We often try and take off in life at full throttle after setting our goals and making all preparations, but if our attitude is not correct, we'll barely be able to leave the ground, or worse, we might even crash into oblivion.

Chapter Four

IT'S ALL ABOUT BALANCE, SON

After practising a few more times I was able to do good take-offs. The exhilaration of leaving the ground and going towards the bright blue sky, where nothing but vast empty space welcomes you is like a favourite aunt saying, "Come and play in my lap for a while, then you can go back to your mother—Mother Earth, in my case."

Every time I took off, I felt like a child who has been rewarded by being allowed to go outside to play after he has finished his lessons.

It was time to learn the finer things. We were flying in the designated practice area and Victor said, "We will first practise acceleration and deceleration and then some turns."

This was music to my ears and I slammed the throttle fully open. The aircraft sprang to life and I was pushed back in my seat. Within seconds, our speed increased from 150 knots to 450 knots. The engine overheat red warning light glowed. The aircraft began to shudder as though it was going to shatter into pieces. Victor got the throttle back and the speed settled to 300 knots. The warning light went off and the aircraft glided smoothly in the sky.

"Ok, reduce the throttle now," he said.

This time, I was careful. I reduced the speed slowly. The speed decreased from 300 knots to 250 knots. I was even more careful as I knew that stall speed was 180 knots. I intended to stop at 200 knots, but before I knew it, the speed went to 180 knots and the aircraft stalled.

Victor took over the controls and recovered it. We lost almost 1,500 feet in the recovery. I was waiting for Victor to yell, to get mad at me. But he was silent. His silence puzzled me. We got back to 5,000 feet.

"Let's practise some turns. Turn 360° with 30° bank, maintain height and speed. You have the controls."

"I have the controls." I was more than eager to impress him. These four words always had an element of magic in them.

Saying them aloud was enough for me to feel powerful and in control, in command.

I started the turn correctly but as the bank increased beyond 20° the speed increased and we started losing altitude.

"Check speed and height," he instructed.

"Yes, Sir," I responded.

By the time I corrected the speed and the height, the bank had increased to 45°. Before I could correct it, we had turned 360°. Not bad at all for the first time, as long as Victor did not have to take over, I consoled myself. Victor had been quiet all along. It upset me a bit. It was time to go back. He took over the controls and we turned towards the airfield.

"You know what is the problem with you?" Victor asked. Thank God he finally said something. Anything he uttered was welcome.

"Did you even notice the ball in the artificial horizon?" He was sure I hadn't. He continued, "The ball must be in the centre to maintain a balanced condition of flying. Let's start with acceleration. You slammed the throttle. This made the aircraft reach its limit too quickly. The engine got overheated and the airframe was juddering. You have to do it in stages, smoothly and deliberately.

"During deceleration, you over-corrected and stalled. You were so shocked that you forgot to recover. When you are with someone, you almost take it for granted that the other person will save you from a situation that you have created.

"During the turns, you forgot that extra power is required to maintain the turn, otherwise you lose height and the speed increases. You focused on one instrument for a long time. Had you checked the ball, you would have noticed that we were slipping in the turn. You had such a beautiful horizon, had you used it, the aircraft would have turned beautifully.

"Now for something personal, you really don't expect too much from yourself. You let the plane take you for a ride and then you try to correct the mistakes. When you say, 'I have the controls', you have the controls over each and every parameter—height, speed, direction, bank, everything. It's all about balance. You cannot look at one parameter and forget the rest.

"Look at your life. Is it in balance? Do you give equal weightage to your personal and professional life? How is your physical health and emotional well-being? Most of us climb the ladder of success only to realise that the ladder is leaning against the wrong wall. A few of us give our best time and energy to our jobs and businesses and one day come back to an empty house. Half of our lives we neglect health to gain wealth and then spend the same wealth to regain the lost health. We have formulated notions of quality time as if two weeks of togetherness in a year compensate for all the days when we didn't have time to listen to our spouse and children. Most of us do not even know the names of our children's friends. In the end, on the deathbed, no one wants more money or material things. All that one wants is more time with their loved ones, family and friends. You are young now. Try and find balance in life and you will be automatically successful. It is all about balance son."

What he said made sense. I would be thinking of his words for a long time.

Chapter Five

IDEALISE, VISUALISE, REALISE (IVR)

Victor had me shaken with his remarks. I confessed to him that I was trying to do my best but didn't know how to. There is comfort in acceptance, more so in front of your coach. There is no harm in letting him know of your weaknesses and shortcomings. Victor was sympathetic and agreed to help.

"Do you visualise?" he asked me.

"Visualise? No, I don't know how to do it, though I've heard of it."

"Okay, this technique is practised by Olympians, athletes, sportsmen and golfers. There are three steps. The first step is to idealise. Imagine your ideal situation. Before every sortie, choose a place where you will not be disturbed. Go and sit there with your eyes closed. Imagine the exact parameters you want to see during each manoeuvre, in the exact sequence… imagine the end result and think how happy and satisfied will you be after the sortie.

"The second step is to visualise. Now, concentrate on the feeling and visualise the entire sortie, right from the start-up, go over the take-off and the complete sortie… visualise the needles of speed, height and bank on the instrument panel exactly as they should be. Visualise with all your senses. Listen to the changes in the sound of the engine when you increase or decrease the speed and imagine the movement of the body with the turns. Feel the satisfaction after you complete each task perfectly. Flying, as living, is all about feeling. What you feel when you visualise is what you will get to feel later.

"The third and final step is to realise. Go for the sorties and realise whatever you have visualised."

He looked at me, and seeing my confused look, he added, "What I would suggest is that you make a Vision Board. Draw the layout of the entire cockpit with all the dials. Make the needles on the dial point to the ideal parameters that you wish to see. Draw the runway as it looks during an ideal landing. Now begin with starting the engine. Move your hands, flick the switches and imagine hearing the sounds of the pumps and the motors. Use all your senses. Smell the turbine fuel as it ignites in the engine, listen to the sound of the propellers, feel the vibration of the cockpit, everything. In the same way, go over the entire sortie, right from take-off to the landing.

"If you want, create a Vision Board at home as well for your life too. Put pictures of yourself and your girlfriend on it. Put up drawings or photographs of your ideal house, and your ideal car. Create a picture of your ideal financial condition. From travel magazines, cut pictures of all those holiday destinations that you wish to visit and paste those on the board. If it is a beach, close your eyes and hear the sound of the waves, smell the salty air, feel the soft sand in your fingers. Get it?"

I nodded, intrigued. He continued.

"Try and feel happy and grateful for it in advance, as though you have already realised your dreams and desires. This might sound a little confusing at first but with a bit of practice, it will be easy to feel gratitude for something that you don't have yet. Feel thankful for it in advance.

"The most important thing is to do IVR without an iota of doubt in your mind. If you believe it will happen, it is sure to happen. If you do it several times but have doubts whether your dreams will come true, you can be sure they won't."

"When is the best time to do this?" I asked.

"Do it preferably at night, just before sleeping. The subconscious mind is powerful, and it works best when we don't interfere with it. Do not worry about how it will all happen. Let the Universe take care of the details while you focus on exactly what you want. It is like sitting in a restaurant and ordering a meal. If you keep changing your order, how is the steward to blame for the delay?"

I listened with full attention, my eager mind wanting to know more.

"Have you seen the movie, Guru?" Victor suddenly asked.

"Yes, it's on the life of the greatest Indian entrepreneur Mr

Dhirubhai Ambani, the founder of Reliance Industries."

"Remember the scene in which he is starting his business and tells his wife to imagine big factories employing thousands of people, a big house and a big car? Later, all that eventually comes true."

"That's right," I answered.

"Sometimes we use IVR without even being aware of the fact, and often for the wrong reasons. Don't you sometimes visualise yourself getting stuck in traffic when you are late and it actually happens? So, if it works for the bad things, why not the good stuff? But you know our greatest enemies are anxiety, worry, fear and doubt. Lack of faith or belief creates anxiety. Anxiety creates worry and doubt. Doubt causes fear. There is a way to change your belief system but more on that later. For now, just do the things I have told you and you will get the results."

Chapter Six

THE FLIGHT OF THE EGO

I took to Victor's teachings the way a fish takes to water,

I started practising IVR regularly and both Victor and I were happy with the results. I was doing perfect landings and take-offs. Once we were coming back from a sortie and we happened to bump into our Chief Instructor, Mitra.

Mitra was a man in his early forties, mid-sized, bespectacled and with a slightly bulging tummy. He had some 20,000 hours on the same aircraft type. He was a master on the trainer aircraft and like all geniuses he was famous for his idiosyncrasies. We had seen him ripping instructors apart during morning briefings. He would not even spare the weathermen with their predictions and more often than not, his predictions were correct. He was equally revered for his professionalism and feared for his temper. He had a mocking tone and his favourite word was 'tch-tch'.

"How are his landings? Is he ready for an early solo, tch-tch?" he asked Victor, referring to me.

Usually, a cadet is required to go solo and fly all alone, after his thirteenth sortie but it can be advanced to after the ninth. I had just finished my ninth. I looked pleadingly at Victor. Nothing is more heartening for a pupil than to know that his instructor or coach has faith in his abilities.

"I think he is ready, Sir," Victor said, smiling proudly at me. I blushed and felt the blood rushing to my face.

"Ok, schedule him with me for a solo-check tomorrow," said Mitra.

I was both happy and apprehensive. The CI was known for his loose hand in the cockpit. Cadets had come out with their masks stained with blood. I was scared, and it showed the next day. More than the dread of being hit by the CI, it was the anxiety of letting Victor down. I was afraid and nervous and my worst fears were realised.

I had barely taxied out when I got a whack on my face. "Is this the taxiing speed? Do you want to take off from the taxi track?"

Mitra took over the controls and got us back.

"Start again," he barked.

Victor, in his own wisdom, had permitted me to taxi fast, but I had forgotten that this was a test and that I would have to be more cautious. I ought not to be in a hurry to finish the ordeal.

As the take-off roll began, I got another one.

"Not centre-line, centre of centre-line," he shouted.

I was told that he was a stickler for perfection. If the required speed was 250 knots, the needle had to be exactly on 250, neither 249 nor 251. The grapevine had it that he could tell you the speed of the aircraft with his eyes closed, just by listening to the sound of the engine.

Before I could settle on down-wind, there was another one, "Who will do the checks?"

By now I was angry and exhausted. I was lagging. I didn't want his hand to come flying towards me and I subconsciously watched out for it. I managed to land properly, I thought, and looked at him for approval, but got some words of censure instead.

"Was that landing or an arrival? You can never become a pilot. We are going back. How did Victor even recommend you?"

More than any physical assault, it was his words that hurt me, more so when he doubted and questioned Victor's judgment.

"I can and I will," I said to myself, under my breath. My fists were clenched.

Victor was waiting for us. He and the CI exchanged a few words privately. I saw Victor smile and felt odd. Anyone could see I was bleeding. How could he smile after all this, I wondered.

He came to me, offered me his handkerchief and said, "You have blood coming from your nose."

I don't know why, but I thought his voice was insincere. I refused his handkerchief and wiped the blood with the sleeve of my overalls.

"Don't worry, you have all the time. We'll get everything right. Cheer up now," said Victor.

The CI had shaken my faith as well as my confidence, but to see Victor smile had almost broken my spirit. I was disappointed in him, to say the least. Was it a set-up? Had both my instructor and Chief Instructor planned this? I was troubled with several questions and filled with doubts about myself, about my abilities, about life and about everything! Suddenly the world had turned upside down.

I knew that pride goeth before a fall, that arrogance and self-pride were sure to bring disappointing results, but I never knew that the fall would feel like this. The pride of going for an early solo-check and the fall of failing it made me feel disgusted with myself. Would I ever make it? I wondered.

We had a spell of bad weather for almost a week. I was standing in front of the flight-plan board as one of my friends made the flying programme. He had scheduled me with Mitra for the solo check again. As per rules, a cadet does the repeat solo check with a different examiner, to avoid bias. As I pointed the anomaly to my friend, I heard Mitra's voice,

"Tch-tch, please get your travel bookings done. At least you can go home comfortably after you have been thrown out of flying."

He was standing right behind us and had heard the entire conversation. The mocking tone made me feel weak and vulnerable.

I talked to my girlfriend Sapna about it when I met her in the park that evening. "This will be our last meeting," I told her very abruptly, without offering any explanation.

She was confused and didn't know what to say. "What's the

matter? Have I done anything?" she asked, confused.

"Nothing, it's got nothing to do with you. If I don't pass the test, I won't show you my face again, the face of a loser," I told her, kicking stones rather viciously as we walked on the grass.

Chapter Seven

SAPNA, MY DREAM

I had met Sapna for the first time during the vacation from the Military Academy, just before I joined the Flying School. It was a pleasant summer evening in 1991. Both of us were visiting our folks who stayed in adjacent houses. I saw Sapna standing on the terrace of her uncle's home, talking animatedly with her cousin Chanda. With her blunt cut hair, she made a pretty though strange sight, an alien in the land of girls with long hair, braided and tied with ribbons.

I'd always told my sisters that I'd never marry a girl with short hair. Neither someone who came from the Armed Forces background nor someone from my own state. I realised that

Sapna fulfilled the other two criteria as well. When we went over to their house, (my cousin Baby and Chanda were good friends and practically lived in each other's homes) and Baby got us talking. The moment our eyes met; I knew that I would have to forget my well-laid plans. For me, it was love at first sight. I had never seen anyone who was so serene, simple and appealing. Her voice was gentle and mellifluous. As she spoke, all I felt was an overwhelming sense of peace. Anyone who has been in love will know what I mean. When you meet the person, you have been dreaming of all your life, you just know it. Statistically, the chances of you meeting your soul mate are one in a billion. The series of coincidences was astonishing.

Sapna's father was posted in the same town where my Flying School was. In passing, she casually mentioned her postal address.

When we got home, I thanked Baby and told her that I would be marrying Sapna one day. She was both amazed and amused.

I have this habit of writing down my thoughts. Some people talk to themselves when they are confused. I write down my thoughts. I tore a page from a notebook and jotted down the pros and cons of marrying Sapna, the girl I was madly in love with, though I had just spoken to her for barely a few minutes. On the reverse of the sheet, I wrote her address.

The next day Baby came and told me, "Hey, Manu, guess what? I met Sapna and told her about your decision to marry her, she's furious. More than her, it's Chanda who is mad at you. They're planning to come over in the evening and give you a piece of their minds."

I was curious to know what Sapna would say. That evening, I watched her from the living room as she walked in, accompanied by Chanda. Her determined stride and her poise made my resolve even stronger, and my heart was beating fast.

"How can you decide so soon, Manish? We've hardly met, we don't even know each other," she accused me.

I was calm. "You know, Sapna, one doesn't have to know someone in order to decide. You can be with a person your whole life and yet remain strangers or you can be with the special one for a mere moment and get the feeling that you've known each other forever."

Sapna's nonchalance clearly indicated that she wasn't impressed.

"I have made my decision and I will wait for you," I said. "In the meantime, we can write to each other and see when you make up your mind."

"You cannot write to her!" Chanda interrupted, like an overprotective, worldly-wise chaperone, in an authoritative voice. I paid no attention to her, but she was bent on making herself heard. "Give back her address!" she almost screamed.

How did Chanda know that I had jotted down Sapna's address? I wondered. Baby must have seen me write it down. I had memorised the address. Better than arguing with Chanda, I fished out the sheet of paper from my pocket and started tearing it up.

Sapna noticed all the writing and asked, "What is all this you've written?"

Before I could reply, she snatched the torn bits from my hand and started reading them. Just then, the lights went off. It was time for the usual weekly load shedding.

As others got busy looking for candles and matches, Chanda who was determined to tarnish my image, chirped, "You must surely have a matchbox, smoker?"

I ignored the insult and struck a match. The room lit up but all I saw was a pair of eyes, shining bright, looking back at me. No one spoke. In the silence and the darkness, two worlds merged into one and a lot was exchanged. The light that reflected from her eyes illuminated the dark dungeons of my soul, it would be the light that would guide me, show me the path in the meandering alleys of life.

"You've burnt your fingers," Sapna exclaimed as she took my hand in hers, throwing away the match.

"I sure have," I said, enjoying the pun. At that moment, all I desired was to hug Sapna, hold her tight, so tight that she would melt like the candle which Baby had lit and placed on the table by then.

As we stared at the candle, a moth got into the flame and met its end.

"Saw that?" I asked.

Like actors on a stage, we had become oblivious to the presence of Baby and Chanda.

**"The desire of the moth for the star,
Of the night for the morrow,
The devotion to something afar
From the sphere of our sorrow."**

I recited the lines as though I was in a trance and Sapna looked at me, hypnotised. Chanda grabbed her hand and took her home.

My cousins got the news very fast, thanks to Baby who wasted no time in such things. "She won't accept you, Manu," they all clucked in false sympathy. "The first heartbreak is very hard to handle."

My heart sank. I believed them.

"A drink will help you drown your sorrows. We'll get you some whiskey, just give us the money."

For them, it was an excuse to have a little fun at my expense and I was an easy prey. It was almost impossible to get money for a drink at that age. I had never touched the panacea of the lovelorn though I could recite Madhushala verbatim and knew its potency.

The whiskey arrived and the bottle was thrust into my hands. In retrospect, I rather enjoyed the feeling of drowning my imaginary miseries and behaved like a tragedy king of Hindi cinema, with a lot of encouragement from my worthy cousins. Before I knew it, I was inebriated. Later, of course, I realised that miseries couldn't be drowned in a drink; alcohol merely irrigates them.

Things worked out for me, as they always do for anybody who knows what they want. A flurry of letters was exchanged between Sapna and me. And one day, I found myself at her doorstep, ready to be interviewed by her father. The movie scene in which an army officer takes out his gun to shoot his daughter's boyfriend repeatedly flashed through my mind. If you have ever done anything scary like bungee jumping, parachuting or even jumping off a 10-metre-high diving board, you will understand the feeling of dread. The fear almost paralyses you when it is your turn to take the Leap of Faith. You take a few deep breaths, shake yourself and take the final step. I did just that: I took a deep breath, braced myself and pressed the doorbell.

The sound of a dog barking didn't help my frayed nerves. The door was answered by Sapna's father who appeared holding Sherry, their pet Pomeranian. He was a man in his mid-forties, fit and muscular for his age like all army men are. Anyone who loves a pet is sure to love a human more, I said to myself, trying to feel better.

"Come inside, son, why are you so scared? Sherry won't bite you," he said, putting his arm around my shoulder.

I wished I could tell him that the fear of the canine was the last thing in my mind and that it was him whom I dreaded meeting. But the warmth of his touch had already made me feel comfortable and my breathing soon returned to normal. Some people have that aura about them, the moment you meet them, you trust them and relax, sure that they will never harm you.

"So, you are the smart young man my daughter has been talking about?" he started, as we settled down in the living room which had trophies, medals, and photographs—proof and a reminder of his achievements in the army.

"Yes Sir, I really love your daughter." I blurted out. I had meant to use the word 'like' but 'love' escaped my lips. There was silence in the room for a few seconds which seemed like an eternity to me. He looked at me intently and then burst out laughing.

"I love her too. Let's drink to that." He got up to fix the drinks and came back with two large glasses of scotch on the rocks.

"Cheers! May you win her over! You know, young man, my daughter is a very strong-headed girl. If you really want her in your life, you will have to be at least as good as me, if not better, both as an officer and as a gentleman, as a professional and as a human being."

"I promise you, Sir, she will always be proud of me."

He consented to my visiting their home, but with the understanding that I would concentrate on my flying and let Sapna focus on her studies. Thus began my slow and steady courtship of Sapna. I was a regular visitor to their house. Sapna's mother was a great cook and pampered me and to a lad who ate his meals in the Mess, it meant a lot.

My dream of becoming a pilot had been a very strong desire but when I met Sapna, it became a burning ambition. There was now an emotional reason. Like any other man, I wanted to please my woman. It's a primordial instinct. Many a successful man will tell you that his ambition is fuelled by his desire to bestow gifts on the woman he loves. Goals, dreams and desires become stronger when emotions are attached to them.

I wanted to be a pilot because I wanted to see Sapna happy. For me, my dream had become our dream. I could feel the pride in her voice whenever she introduced me to her friends, saying, "He is at the Flying School. Very soon he will fly me in his plane."

But now it was all going to change.

Chapter Eight

FIGHT TO FLY

I knew that if I failed the test, my flying career would end and her parents would look for someone else for her. She was my age and they were in a hurry to get her married. Becoming a pilot was the quickest way for me to get a job, and from the look of it, this was likely to get delayed.

It's strange, but when you think that your life's most precious dream is about to shatter, everything else follows. Your whole life, like a house of cards, seems to crumble and come crashing down as well. It is like a chain reaction, a domino effect, with one catastrophe following the other.

At the depth of despair, you accept the inevitable and as you wallow in despondency and self-pity, you start to rationalise, you ration your lies. Think about it, whenever you have to provide an excuse for something, it is only for failure. No one makes excuses for success. So, there I was, thinking that maybe failure was good for me, that it was my destiny… I am the only son of my parents and would probably be able to help them better if I was not a pilot… I might have died in a plane crash… blah, blah, blah…

Whenever I was confused and unable to think straight, I wrote down my thoughts. I wrote to Polly who was my confidante and had always been supportive. When I would unburden my heart to Polly, she would reply. Her letters were a constant source of encouragement, showing me the light when everything seemed bleak and dark clouds of doom loomed large on my horizon. This time, the clouds were the darkest.

I have known Polly since we were children. She was my friend's cousin. It all began with our trips to the wildlife sanctuary. Her father was a Forest Ranger, a jovial man, always smiling and full of encouragement. Her brother, Manu, and I became friends. My short name was Manu as well. We shared a special affinity with each other. On these trips, Manu taught me how to flip stones on lake beds and I was the only kid who had the privilege of handling his expensive camera.

Polly was studying in a good school and aspired to become a writer. She read voraciously, spoke well and had clarity of thought even back then. Since early childhood, I have been fascinated with books, words and writers. I was twelve and asked Polly to help me improve my English. She asked me to write letters to her, which she promised to correct and send back to me. This was the pre-internet era and letter-writing was a way of life. Thus began our regular correspondence with each other. We exchanged letters and greeting cards. Polly's birthday card would be the first to arrive each year. It meant a lot to a kid who studied in a boarding school during a time when letters were a lifeline, the only means to stay in touch.

It was the morning of the 25th of February, my seventeenth birthday. I had been waiting for my birthday card from Polly. I usually received them well in advance. She had never been this late in sending it. It arrived late that afternoon, with a little handwritten note: "Sorry for the delay. I know you must be waiting. With deep grief, I write of the death of Bhaiya on Friday the 13th of February."

I was shocked at the news and touched by the fact that Polly had remembered to send me birthday wishes. Could a person overcome his or her personal grief just to make someone happy? I wondered what I ought to do. The next day, I received a letter from my parents informing me about the tragedy.

Manu had gone to see off a friend at the railway station. As he ran alongside the moving train, he slipped and fell in the narrow space between the train and the platform. He died on the spot and his body was mutilated beyond recognition. The police found his wallet and contacted his family.

Polly's mother was not allowed to see the remains of her son's body as there was nothing to see. She was in disbelief and insisted that it was the body of some pickpocket who had robbed her son, and that Manu was still alive. I decided to go and meet her. I boarded a bus for their town and arrived at their home in a few hours. It was Polly who opened the door.

"Who is it, Polly?" her mother asked from the other room.

"It's Manu," Polly replied.

"Manu? See, my son is alive, didn't I tell you all that he is alive?"

Polly's mother came running to the door and saw me standing there.

"Oh, it' is you!" she exclaimed in disappointment and collapsed on the floor, sobbing uncontrollably.

I felt so awkward and embarrassed that I wished I had never come. I would never have imagined that my presence would cause so much pain to someone. For a clumsy teenager, such situations were tough to handle. I had no savoir-faire to comfort her, either with words or with a gesture. As Polly's mother wept in grief, I couldn't help but cry. I noticed that Polly was composed and her eyes were dry. I wondered why. I was too young to understand many things.

After a while, her father arrived. With his usual cheerful smile, he said, "So how is my young pilot? When do I get to fly with you?"

I was puzzled. Here was a man who had just lost his son and he still managed to smile. Sensing my confusion, he said, sighing, "It happens, son. Life goes on."

Polly called me upstairs for tea. She began talking and filled me in with details of her brother's death. "You know, Manu, I didn't have the time to cry." Saying this, she broke down. I guess her pent-up sorrow found an outlet at last. Once again, I felt embarrassed and didn't know what to say at such a time.

Once I went back to school, I wrote a sympathetic letter to Polly's parents. I was quite expressive while communicating through written correspondence. I even wrote to Polly saying that she could henceforth look upon me as her brother.

"I had only one brother and he is no more now, I hope you understand," she wrote back. I was a little perplexed by her reply but respected her decision. Polly never addressed me as 'Manu' after that again.

Coming back to the present, I was sure I was about to fail the solo check and thought that quitting at that juncture would be a good idea. I got all my excuses together and wrote a letter to Polly saying that I had made a conscious decision to quit so that my self-esteem was salvaged. I was amazed at my ability to justify my actions of becoming a coward, of giving up on my dream without a fight, giving up on what was closest to my heart, my *raison d'être*, my reason to live.

So, this is how a person behaves when he suffers from 'excusitis'. He has an excuse for everything, for not taking action when he knows he should. This is the loser's way. I hated myself for it but I had made up my mind, I had resigned myself to the fact that I was destined for failure. I had prepared myself for it so that it didn't hurt me when it actually happened. I was ready to embrace it. I somehow appreciated myself for having come to terms with life so easily. I had seen the feeble-hearted cry, packing their bags when they were thrown out of flying, I was strong; there would be no tears for me, thank you.

Prepared with my new-found thinking, I nonchalantly sat in the cockpit for probably the last sortie before my solo check. In my wisdom, I had even applied for a change of instructor. I was assigned to Matthews. Matthews was a man with a perpetual smile on his face. He was the youngest instructor. We were witness to his predicament during the morning briefings. Mitra would humiliate him and insult him in front of all of us whenever Matthew fumbled or replied unsatisfactorily to Mitra's nagging queries. Once, Mitra even stopped his lecture halfway on the pretext that he was ill-prepared. Matthews never contradicted Mitra. He would nod his head in agreement and humbly accept all the lacerations. The smile never left his lips.

To give me maximum time, Matthew did a short take-off and placed me on the final approach for landing. I was doing things mechanically; I just wanted to finish the sortie. Harshly manipulating the controls, I almost forced the plane to go down.

"Watch your speed! Do you plan to crash it to the ground?" said Matthew a little harshly.

He took over the controls and again placed me on the final approach. Before I knew it, he had whacked me squarely on my mask, "Who will land the *****ing plane?"

I was surprised at his behaviour and his tone. I managed to land it. Flying with his left hand, he lashed out at me once again.

"What's wrong with you? The next sortie is your final solo check and you are not even flying with your usual concentration."

I had nothing to lose now. I had not planned to be beaten up on my last day in the air. As they say, one should never kick a man when he has fallen down. And I was being punched before being kicked out of flying. What an irony! But I was not going to take it lying down!

He got me on the finals again, "You have the controls, show me one good landing."

"Sir, you have the controls. I'm not feeling well." I gave him the ultimate excuse.

"Come on, two more landings and we are done." Until then, Matthew had been landing the plane and opening the throttle, he was getting a bit frustrated.

I pressed the 'talk' button and asked permission from the tower to taxi back. He was shocked at my action but he relented.

"What's wrong with you? Why are you behaving like this?" he asked.

We were on our way back to the parking area. I narrated to him the entire episode with Mitra. I told him that Mitra had made up his mind to bounce me, to fail me in the solo check and that I had resigned myself to my fate. I had decided to quit.

"Freshen up and come to my cabin. We'll talk. You should have told me the whole thing earlier," he said as we switched off.

Soon, I was with him in his cabin.

"You know, Manish, a lot of people give up when they are just one step short of success. If I know you well, you have dreamed of becoming a pilot all your life. Are you going to give up just because somebody else does not have faith in your abilities because somebody else does not want you to succeed? Look at me! Haven't you seen Mitra humiliate and lacerate me in public? Have I given up?"

I looked at him and saw tears in his eyes, the tears when one is a witness to a life being reduced to mediocrity, when one hears the sound of dreams and hopes shattering. It is contagious. I felt as though they were my tears, tears that I had been holding back.

"I only request you to put up a good fight, to do your best. Let Mitra know what type of a pilot you are and want to be.

Even if he has made up his mind, let him regret it. Let his conscience prick him if he decides to fail you. I am sorry I hit you. But I could not let you give up on yourself, because I know your worth."

As he spoke, something snapped inside me. Before I realised it,

I was sobbing uncontrollably. There was something still left in me that began to take over and become strong. Like adrenaline injected into a dead soul.

Someone came and handed me a pink envelope. It was a letter from Polly. I was surprised. The postal service was unusually prompt. I intuitively knew what she must have replied. Help always seem to arrive at the right time. It was as though the whole Universe was getting into some sort of conspiracy to prevent me from giving up and to help me succeed. Matthew asked me to read the letter. I read it:

"…As far as I can remember, Manish, you have always talked of becoming a pilot, but now when you are faced with an obstacle, you are ready to give up, accepting quick defeat. It is your life, of course, but also always remember that it is you who are choosing to quit. You have taken the decision and you have to be comfortable with it all your life. Where death is concerned, read these lines by Jack London…"

"I would rather be ashes than dust. I would rather my spark should burn out in a brilliant blaze than that it should be stifled by dry rot. I would rather be a superb meteor, every atom of me in a magnificent glow than a sleepy and permanent planet. The proper function of man is to live. I shall not waste my days trying to prolong them. I shall use my time."

As I read the letter again, my tears flowed freely, breaking the barrage that had been held back so strongly. My vision got blurred. Matthew was watching it all. He put an arm around my shoulder and said, "Cheer up now, Manish, and get ready for the sortie. Just get ready for your solo."

I felt a lot better. With the newfound will and determination, I pulled myself together and made an attempt to smile. How could I have let myself become an object of self-pity, I wondered.

As we walked in the corridor, we heard Mitra. He was walking right behind.

"Is he ready for his solo check?"

We both looked back and he was staring into my face. I was sure he knew what had happened. The control tower must have informed him that we had returned before having finished the sortie. I dreaded whatever was to come.

"How is he feeling now?" he asked Matthew. Without waiting for the answer, he asked me, "Do you have a fag?"

I fumbled in my pockets for some cigarettes.

"Let's walk," he suggested.

I handed him the packet. He lit a cigarette and held the lit match. "You can also light up, you'll feel better."

We smoked in silence. I glanced at his face, trying to fathom his thoughts. He had a faraway look on his face. Known for his tricky behaviour, I wondered if this was all some kind of drama before the curtains finally fell on my flying career.

"Finish your sortie with Matthew and do not switch off. We'll fly in the same plane," he said, stubbing the butt with his flying boots.

I watched him. To me, it was like somebody squashing my dreams. The lines of a poem by William Butler Yeats reverberated in my whole being:

"But I, being poor, have only my dreams;

 I have spread my dreams under your feet,

Tread softly because you tread on my dreams."

I shook myself up, like a boxer getting up before the count of ten, for the final round.

I flew with Matthew. We had already done thirty minutes. We still had fifteen minutes left. Matthew was pleased with my performance. When we stopped, we waited for Mitra.

"Remember what I told you. Just have faith in your own abilities and don't worry about the consequences. Relax, I will send Mitra," said Matthew.

I waited for Mitra in the cockpit. A part of me felt like a lamb at the end of a rope, trapped in a cage waiting to be devoured by a lion. The other part was the brave sheep ready to fight till the end, for his right, his right to freedom and a wonderful life. Now, which of these two represented my true self, I wondered. I remembered a story that my mother used to narrate.

Once, a lion cub was lost in the jungle. He was found by a sheep mother who adopted him and reared him as her own lambs. The cub was raised with the lambs, eating grass with them, bleating like them, running away and hiding when they heard the lion's roar or when they saw other predators. The cub and the lambs grew up. One day, as usual, when they heard a lion, all the sheep started running for their lives, the young lion ran too, but he soon stopped. As he listened, something stirred inside him, something that was waiting to be awakened. He opened his mouth and let out a full roar. The jungle reverberated with the new roar. He had become a lion and he could not return to being a sheep ever again.

"Are you ready, Manish?" Mitra's mocking voice jolted me out of my thoughts.

"I am ready for you, Sir!" There was a roar in my voice which caught me unawares, surprising me pleasantly. I knew it. It was a turning point, the moment of truth, the moment when a child becomes a man. It was a spiritual awakening, the moment when one becomes aware of the powers that lie untapped within oneself, within one's higher self.

Mitra signalled to me to taxi as he strapped himself in the seat and connected his headphones.

"Examiner 02, taxi," I said. There was the same roar in my voice. So, it is permanent, I mused.

"Clear to taxi and our best wishes."

In the small, well-knit community, almost everyone knows everything. The Air Traffic Controllers at the tower had a fair enough idea of my predicament. Everyone cheers when the knocked-out boxer gets up before the count, when David stands before a Goliath, ready to claim his destiny.

It feels good when people are there to cheer for you. Everyone likes a winner, especially when he is the underdog. As I taxied, I could feel their good wishes paving the way for my success. When I stopped before entering the runway to carry out vital actions and checks before take-off, I noticed the look of approval on Mitra's face. My hands flew magically over the switches and the words flowed perfectly from my lips like mantras at a yagna— a priest performing a religious ceremony.

I was in the flow, in the 'now'. I noticed the heightened presence, the sense of awareness. Performing the last part of the checks, I verified the wind speed and looked at the windsock. I felt it waving its good wishes gently to me at 5-8 knots in the direction of take-off, perfect for flying. I thought of the old saying:

'Winds and waves always favour the ablest navigators.'

After a perfect line-up, I opened the throttle, holding the aircraft on brakes. I saw Mitra shuffle comfortably in his seat, as one does before witnessing a performance. I also, as an accomplished performer, released the brakes for the first act. The aircraft charged ahead like an obedient horse, maintaining direction perfectly. I was amazed; I had not even struggled for it. **I realised that giving up the struggle was the key.** I was doing everything effortlessly, without being concerned about the result. I was doing everything to the best of my ability, and I was detached from the outcome.

"What a take-off, Manish! Perfect!" Mitra commended.

I wasn't quite sure whether he was praising me or mocking me, but I wasn't affected. There comes a time in everybody's life when bouquets or brickbats fail to bother. I was only concerned about flying the best 45 minutes of my life, every minute the very best, for this could well be my last 45 minutes in the air.

The poem '*If*' by Rudyard Kipling summed up my feelings at that moment:

"If you can fill the unforgiving minute
With sixty seconds' worth of distance run -
Yours is the Earth and everything that's in it,
And - which is more - you'll be a Man, my son!'
The landing was even better.
"Show me two more like this."

Usually, the examiner or the instructor takes over controls during the roller take-offs, when the plane does a continuous take-off after landing.

Mitra's hands were on the top of instrument panels, tapping his fingers, and playing his favourite *tabla* music. He gestured to me to continue.

"Roller take-offs as a cadet, wow!"

Was he still playing games with me? Tantalizing me? Doubts started creeping up again. **When faith crumbles questions crop up.** I wasn't too sure. My newfound faith in myself and my abilities was not too strong. It was being tested. It is so easy to fall back into the same trap of self-doubt, even if things seem to be better.

It was my third landing. Mitra hadn't touched the controls once nor uttered a word. He just sat there tapping his fingers and humming an old tune. Was he letting me play because it was my last time in the cockpit? I wondered. As I landed, he signalled to me to clear the runway.

Where should I go? If I went straight, it would take me to the dispersal where the aircraft were parked and that would have meant the end of everything. If I turned right, it would take me to the beginning of the runway for my solo.

This time, it was the voice of the controller on the radio, "Clearing off, confirm?"

I had friends in the ATC. They were spectators anxiously awaiting the results of a nail-biting finish of the match which seemed to be ending in a draw.

"Affirm." Continuing the suspense, Mitra played to the gallery.

I had the controls and I stopped at the intersection without his instructions. Unlike Robert Frost and his 'Road Not Taken' I wanted to travel the 'road most taken'. I wanted to give him the time to decide my fate, for his conscience to prick him. I had decided that even if the decision would be against me, I would not plead or beg.

When Alexander defeated Porus, he asked him how he wished to be treated. "Like a king," Porus replied.

And here, there was a victor and a probably soon-to-be-vanquished, but one determined to maintain his dignity and self-respect.

Chapter Nine

YOU ARE ON YOUR OWN

"Examiner 02, call sign changed to 120. Clearing off to holding point for Runway 09"

The Controller almost shouted, "Go!"

"Congratulations, 120. You are clear," said the Controller.

Everything happened so suddenly that I nearly missed it. It was euphoric, almost dream-like. I was in a daze for a moment. We stopped and Mitra got out of the cockpit. Standing on the wings, he secured his seat and strapped the parachute. He asked me, "Were you sure of clearing the solo check?"

"Yes Sir, I was, but not with you," I replied, looking into his eyes, summoning all my courage.

"The country needs pilots like you," he said. This time, his mocking tone was missing.

As is customary, the pilot handing over the plane goes around it to check for any abnormalities. Mitra walked around, coming over to the other side, lifting the visor of his helmet, he said, "You are on your own, son." He then showed me the all ok thumbs up sign and saluted.

The salute is a gesture of respect to a worthy colleague, a welcome to the League of Legends, to the group of special people who not only face death every day but mock it, and to people who are willing to lay down their lives for their motherland. There is no gesture which depicts admiration and devotion better than a salute. Salute, I salute thee. So many times you have been used to show respect and reverence to the flag and to the worthy men.

"120 line-up," I asked for permission to enter the runway.

Looking at the empty seat next to mine, the memories of my childhood days were replayed. I was 11 years old. When my parents took a siesta during the summer afternoons, I would often sneak out with their second-hand car and drive it to the nearby field to practise my skills. I learnt to drive on my own.

All that had probably helped me today. Everything you learn —all the books you read, all the people you meet, all the interactions you have prepares you for some grand event, some great moment, and this was my moment.

When you are in the flow, in the 'now', everything merges. You become a part of everything and everything becomes a part of you. I have always believed it. For me, my car was as alive as me. I have always been able to relate to it, more as a person rather than an inanimate piece of machinery. Since the beginning, I used to talk with her, plead with her in the winter mornings to start up, and later thank her after a long, rough ride. Now it was a plane. I thanked her for flying so beautifully till then.

"Let's go, baby."

She was my girlfriend and today was my date, my tryst, with destiny.

As I settled after the take-off, an overwhelming sense of peace and bliss engulfed me. There is something in the air, when you are all alone in a small plane for the first time, with the sky above and the earth below, it is when you merge into the vast nothingness that you realize how insignificant and yet how powerful you are.

The first solo is just one landing and it was done perfectly.

As I switched off, I saw a small crowd gathered in the dispersal. At the head of the crowd were Mitra, Victor and Matthew. Mitra came forward and I instinctively bent down to touch his feet. He sensed it and hugged me instead. During that silent moment, a lot was communicated, and a bond was formed. All that I had previously disliked in him vanished. I had only respect for him now. I glanced at Victor. He stood with his arms outstretched beaming with pride. Next to him was Matthew, wiping a tear. After hugging them, it was the turn of my friends. Dudu, as usual, quietly took my helmet from my hand. After the high fives and pats on the back, Mitra asked me to come to his office.

Chapter Ten

A LESSON IN HUMILITY

It was there, in Mitra's office, that the conspiracy was revealed. Only this time the world had conspired for someone to succeed.

The instructors or the Masters have the knack and the nose to sense everything. I was good at flying. I knew it. But what I did not know was that I was becoming overconfident bordering on to conceit.

There is a very thin line between professional pride and arrogance. One begins to lose humility and humbleness when, after having learnt from the Masters, one starts competing with them. Initially, one does not do it consciously, but very soon it becomes an attitude that must be nipped in the bud.

Mitra began, "You know, son, what keeps a man successful?"

"Hard work, professionalism, such things…," I replied.

"No, that's what makes a man successful," he interrupted, "what keeps him successful is his humility and his humbleness. Not only do we want a pilot who is professional, but also one who is humble. I know you did not do it intentionally, but very soon you realised that flying was as easy as driving a car. Flying has another dimension, especially combat flying. Unlike driving, flying is about perfection.

"A successful person is the one who knows that he will never achieve perfection but he strives for it nevertheless. He is eager to learn not just from his Master, but from everyone. For him, it is an unending quest. An unquenchable thirst for knowledge. And a man who is learning is humble. There is humility in the tone of his voice and his manners are genteel. He attains grace.

"Flying is not a skill. It is an art. It is a passion for perfection. It is not only about take-offs and landings but a whole lot in between. Soon after you started doing take-offs and landings on your own, you were only interested in clearing the early solo check. It was your way to show others that you were better than them. Don had sensed it. So, along with Matthew, we planned the entire episode. We wanted to take you to the point where all that you wanted to do was fly but still be detached from the result."

He then related his favourite story:

One of the pupils of Socrates told him that he had a desire to attain wisdom. So, one day Socrates took him to the river and asked him to see his own reflection in the water. As the pupil was peering down, Socrates held his head and pushed it underwater. The pupil struggled to get free to catch his breath. After a few seconds that must have seemed like an eternity to the pupil, Socrates released him. The pupil came up sputtering, very angry, his ego bruised. Socrates asked him, "What was the only thing you desired when you were underwater?" The pupil replied, "To breathe, of course." Socrates then said, "The day your desire to attain knowledge is just as strong, you will have wisdom, my son."

I rubbed my chin pensively.

"So, Manish, what did you want the most during the solo check?"

"Sir, I just wanted to fly."

"It's true that at that time, you were not bothered about the others. You just wanted to fly and fly as perfectly as you could. You did just that, you flew flawlessly. You know, in everybody's life there comes a time when he questions the meaning of his existence. He doubts if his dreams are worth a lifetime of pursuit. Before he gets it all, his resolve is sometimes tested. Anyway, congratulations on not letting yourself down, more so on becoming a man, a humble man."

Later I got to know about the other side of Mitra. Not only was he a professionally qualified pilot but also an extremely patriotic man. I am sure that instead of just red, in his blood, the colours of the country's flag flowed through his veins.

He once asked me, "What is a country? Is it an area marked on the map or defined by geographical boundaries?"

Before I could answer he continued, "Tch-tch, most of us get it wrong. A country is a feeling. A country is not an area with geographical boundaries, it is the feeling you associate with it. It is the feeling when you hear the national anthem or watch the tricolour unfurl or meet your countrymen abroad. You know, we got our independence very cheap. It was a handful of people who set us free from the clutches of our rulers. That is why we take for granted the freedom that we enjoy today.

"Also, if you are in the services, you are in the business of serving. When you are serving, you do not expect anything in return. If you get paid for it or if you have perks attached, it is an added bonus. Remember, it was you who has chosen to serve. So if you are in the services wearing a uniform or in the service industry, the rule is to obey, serve, love, and serve some more. Whether it is your countrymen or your customers, the first thing is to cultivate an attitude of serving with a loving spirit. Sometimes we slip into an attitude of high-handedness thinking that if we have chosen to serve, we are a superior lot and others should recognize our sacrifices. You may expect it, but remember, you cannot demand it. For you, it is Nishkam Seva, serving without expecting any rewards. *Karmanye Wadhikaraste Ma Faleshu Kadachana,* **you only have a right to duty and not to the result."**

I gradually built rapport with Mitra and started flying more frequently with him. Both of us looked for an opportunity to be together in the air. The glass cockpit turned into a classroom, thousands of feet up in the air, away from the hustle and bustle of the earth.

On one of these sorties, he asked me, "Do you know, Manish, what keeps pilots safe and alive? More than their flying acumen, it is their highly developed sixth sense."

I had heard the cliché about common sense being the best sense and told him so.

"No, son, common sense has more to do with instinct but intuition is something different. It is Extra Sensory Perception—ESP. Knowing things before they actually happen. Apart from the five senses of touch, smell, taste, sight and hearing, we are born with the sixth sense of intuition or premonition. If you remember your childhood, you will find instances of having experienced it. Seeing the very same questions you thought of in your question paper or the exact marks you dreamed about. It happens even now, you think of a song and someone begins to hum it. You think of a friend and he or she calls you or shows up. Similarly, most pilots have a heightened sense of premonition, of something that may happen which alerts and prepares them for future contingencies."

"Does this apply just to pilots or to others too?" I enquired.

"Ask any successful person. They will admit that they frequently listen to and use their sixth sense. They sense a deal coming through or a certain feeling about a product or a person. They will also tell you that they have benefited immensely when they paid heed to this sense and suffered losses while disregarding their intuition. This happens when the ego or emotions come in the way."

"Are some people blessed with more of these extraordinary powers than others?" I was more than willing to learn. If I could hone my intuitive powers, it would be fun to know the questions in advance or to know the winning lottery numbers.

"Tch-tch, did you know how to swim or to ride a bike at birth? However, you never doubted learning these skills, right? You always had the belief that if others could learn it, so could you. You had been swimming in your mother's womb since your inception. Later, you had to only remember it. Similarly, you have been using your sixth sense. You have often sensed the presence of your mother, and you have intuitively known her moods, right? Your mother also knew when you were hungry, wet or cold. But as you grew up, the world taught you that these are extraordinary powers and only a very few blessed ones could possess them. If you feel that you are blessed, you will surely be blessed with these powers."

Mitra had a way with words and it always left me intrigued and occasionally frustrated. He loved to tease me with new ideas. Was this his way to test my thirst for the wisdom that he wanted to share with me?

"Sir, will you please teach me how to develop my intuition or sixth sense?" I almost pleaded.

He chuckled, "You are always in a hurry to learn. I like your hunger for knowledge but detest your impatience. Let me tell you a story."

We were ferrying the aircraft to the repair depot. Mitra had suggested that I be his co-pilot. We had to check our position en route and make a few mandatory calls and there was enough time for a story.

Mitra began. "Once upon a time, God felt bored in heaven, so He created the feminine form, the Goddess. Both were equally powerful. They could do everything, become anybody, and could have anything they wished. They devised and played their own games but since they were equals in all respects, the game always ended in a tie. If, for instance, they played hide-and-seek, both had intuitive powers and each one always knew where the other was hiding. Life became boring once again, so He created a few more Gods and Goddesses in His own image. All were equally powerful, omnipotent, omnipresent and omniscient. With the increase in numbers, it was more fun. There were more people to talk to, and more to play with. But the problem remained the same. After dividing them into two teams, neither side won. They played very hard but the game always ended in a draw.

So, God devised a new game on the hide-and-seek theme.

"He declared all the rules: 'All of you, for the sake of the game, will lose all your powers. You will put on masks. With the masks on, you will not be able to recognise yourselves, who you are, and all the powers that you have. Nor will you be able to recognise others. You will all be going to a place called Earth with your masks on. The aim of the game is to recognise yourselves, regain your powers and recognise others. You will have enough indicators in the form of Gurus, Masters, books and instances to teach you who you actually are and why you are there on Earth. As soon as you regain your powers by realising your true selves, you will come and rejoin me in Heaven. If you wish, you will be sent back to Earth to guide and help others. So let the game begin.'"

"I think I know what you're trying to say, but go on, nevertheless," I commented.

Mitra threw me a long quizzical look, through his visor but said nothing. The silence helped the wisdom sink in. It was the moment of awakening.

"All of us are Gods, all of us are as powerful as we want to be," I stated.

"Yes, all of us are Gods, you are one too, if you choose to be. You know, it might take you some time to realise it or it can be satori. Do you know what *SATORI* is?"

As usual, without waiting for my answer, he continued.

"*Satori* is the Zen Buddhist term for instantaneous awakening or transformation. You know, there is a difference between change and transformation. Transformation is a permanent change. If you freeze water to -273° C, it will never get back to liquid form. Similarly, there will be a moment in your life when you will be transformed forever, when you will awaken to your true self, to who you truly are. This happens in a moment and when it happens, it is **SATORI**.

"If you choose, this story could be the *satori* for you."

"On a more practical note, there are a few steps to hone your sixth sense. To begin with, you have to re-train your five senses and sharpen them. Ever been with people who are visually challenged? They almost see with their ears. They develop a databank of sounds and just as we recognise places or things on seeing them, they refer to their databank of sounds to recognise them."

"You know, there was this guy called Ramchand who had lost his eyesight and was employed in one of our offices. I used to offer him a lift in my car whenever I saw him walking home. After a few times, Ramchand told me that he could differentiate between the sound of my car and that of others. He intuitively knew if it was me or my driver who was driving. He had to go somewhere just once and the next time he would find his way there without difficulty. Also, he had developed a heightened sense of touch. His fingers could read and tell him many things."

"So, the first step is to focus on all your senses one by one. You can begin with sight. There is a difference between looking and seeing. Remember, the one who looks outside, dreams; the one who sees within awakens. See the different shapes, angles, colours, lights, reflections, transparency, translucence and opaqueness of objects. See with a different focus. Focus your gaze on the distant horizon and shift inwards to the tip of your nose. See with your peripheral vision. All this while, try to negate the inputs coming from your other senses while you focus on the sense of sight."

"Do likewise with all the other senses. Hear all the sounds, the distant sound of the traffic, the hum of the air conditioner, the sound of your breath and also of your heartbeat. Feel the hard floor, the soft cushion of the chair, the texture of your clothes. Smell the various fragrances. While eating, stop and savour the tastes of various foods and beverages. When you have done it for a few days in continuation, you will notice that you can see more details. Colours and shades will become more vibrant. Shapes will appeal to you. You will begin to see patterns and ratios. Similarly, you will be able to hear, smell, taste and feel more accurately."

"That sounds easy enough," I said.

"The next step is to cross-train your senses. Hear the colours. See the music. Taste the fragrance. Smell the various tastes. Blind painters use this technique."

I looked at him. "How is that possible?" I exclaimed.

"I know it sounds a little bizarre, but you have to first master the former steps and only then will you be able to control the latter."

"But what has all this got to do with developing the sixth sense? We started with that, remember?"

"Can a child learn to run before he is able to walk?"

Mitra seemed a bit annoyed with my impatience.

"Begin using your five senses first, the ones you are already used to, and the sixth will soon re-develop. After some time, you can start using the sixth one too. Has it ever happened that you think of someone, and you receive their call? You cook a little extra in case someone drops in and a friend actually does. You place an extra bottle of water in your car, and it comes in handy. Keep track of all these coincidences, the more you notice them, the more they will occur. At the end of the day, write them down in a little notebook. As you perfect the senses, you will be able to create coincidences.

"Let's suppose that you smell the aroma of coffee and it reminds you of the last time you went to a café with your fiancée. If you wish it would happen again, it will manifest sooner than you expect. Or if it is a song, you want her to hear. The song will play on the radio when you turn it on. And when your wishes are granted, all you must do is to feel grateful."

"Yes, I know about the power of gratitude," I nodded.

"Let's go a step further. When you focus totally on only one of your senses, isolating the others, you would have achieved 'present moment awareness.' You will be fully present. You will be far away from the regrets of your past or the anxieties of the future. In the 'now', your body becomes a vehicle or a medium of intuition. A lot has been discovered about cellular intelligence. Thinking is not restricted to the brain cells alone. All the other cells in the body communicate too. If you listen to your body, it can help you stay fit and help you get rid of your doubts."

Both Mitra and Victor were voracious readers and thinkers. They were well-read and were happy to share their knowledge with me. I am grateful for the wisdom and insights that I received from them. They were my Gurus in more sense than one.

Chapter Eleven

WHERE ARE YOU? ARE YOU ON TRACK?

Time was fleeting. Before I realized it, we had entered the navigation stage.

Victor said, "The first rule is to always know where you are and where you are going. The questions you should always ask yourself are:

"Where am I?

How did I get here?

Where do I need to be?

How do I get back on track?

Am I early or late?

When will I reach my destination?"

"Three things that will help you answer these questions are your map, your compass and your clock. More often than not, you will have a choice of destination, so choose your destination well. You should be sure of what you expect to see at the destination, be it weather, fuel or other services.

"The second rule is to mark your destination in bold on the map. Choose a comfortable cruise speed. Too high will not only strain the engine but will also need extra fuel. Go too slow and you might stall. Choose your waypoints and mark them with time. They will be a measure of your speed: early or late. And most importantly, know your map like the back of your hand. With a glance outside, you should know exactly where you are."

All these rules and methods were getting a bit too much for me. I wondered how migratory birds fly thousands of miles to reach their destination without maps, compasses and clocks. For that matter, any bird. Birds don't have roads, road signs or house numbers to guide them. There must be something more. There has to be some internal reference system which they intuitively use and know how to reach where they have to. Also, I've never heard of a mid-air bird collision. Wouldn't it be better if our cars and planes were fitted with the same intelligence, the same internal radar? We would have a smooth, efficient flow of traffic and there would be no accidents. Are birds better equipped than us? Is our claim of being a better species true?

"What are you thinking?" Victor's voice interrupted my thoughts.

"I'm lost!" I blurted out.

"What?"

"I mean what do I do if I'm lost in the air, if I don't know where I am?"

"Firstly, there should never be a situation in which you are lost. If ever you feel you are lost, have asked all the questions, and still can't make out where you are, then the first rule is 'Do not panic'. The second rule is 'Ask for help'. Just contact anybody and everybody and tell them your last known position."

"Isn't it a bit embarrassing to tell the world that I'm lost?" I asked.

"Yes, it is, but a lost you is better than a dead you. You know, the best of pilots get lost. The reason they are alive is that they let go of their ego, swallowed their professional pride and asked for help, learning precious lessons. They have been helped by complete strangers. Sometimes, some radar unit came on just at the right time, a ham radio operator or a fellow pilot from another country.

"Now, the other tool after the map is the compass. Keep your compass tuned to the magnetic compass. If you do not check it at regular intervals, it will drift away and show you a wrong reading. By 1 in 60 rule, a 1° error will shift you 1 nautical mile from your track after 60 nautical miles."

"Similarly, you must always remember to keep your internal compass tuned to your heart's longings. If you let it astray, it will be pointing towards the wrong star. If you do not choose a direction, you will be drifting in life, like a ship without a rudder."

"The importance of time in life and in flight cannot be over-emphasized. Every second counts. Time is the only commodity you cannot regain. Once it is gone, it is gone forever. Your clock is like your third eye. Whatever you see, you should have an eye on the time. The more you respect time, in time others will respect you. More often than not, we disregard the value of a second. It is these seconds that make a minute. So, do a little exercise now —watch the watch! Do you have a watch?"

I nodded my head in affirmation.

"Just watch the second's hand for one complete rotation, for one complete minute."

I started. Initially, the needle seemed to move fast, but slowly five seconds seemed so long, then even one second seemed a long moment. For the second hand to complete one rotation seemed an eternity.

"So, now you know how long a minute is? When you are airborne, not only do you have to follow time, but you also have to be ahead of time. You do not have to be a slave of time; you must master time. You know, it is us humans who invented time but now we have become its slaves. Time is an illusion. It can be stretched or shortened on demand. When you played the game 'watch your watch', what you did while observing the hand move was that you stretched time. Similarly, you can shorten it."

I wondered how one could do that.

"Don't you have a girlfriend?" Victor asked me.

"Yes Sir," I replied sheepishly.

"Ah, yes, Sapna... Tell me, when you are with Sapna, doesn't time seem to fly? Hours spent with her seem like minutes, right?"

"That's absolutely correct," I chuckled.

"Similarly, in the air, when you are lost or if you have an emergency, every second will feel like an hour. Every second you waste will take you further away from your destination or closer to your death. So, a word of advice for you. **Start treating time as your most precious commodity. You can get back almost anything but not lost time.**"

This was something I committed to memory, it's a lesson I have never forgotten even today.

Chapter Twelve

I AM LOST

Flying at night has its own pleasures and challenges. I love driving at night too. Everything is cool, calm and quiet. Given a choice, I'd rather drive long distances at night. I don't know about others but night driving is no bother for me. Lights can tell you so much! With the lights you know which vehicles are following you on bends and turns, and you can see the lights of approaching vehicles and know you are not alone. When I was a child and we would travel by bus between cities, I'd notice the bus drivers flicker their headlights to signal to one another that the road ahead was clear.

You dim your lights to low beams while crossing each other.

(No one waves at strangers during the day) For me, it is a sign of courtesy to the fellow traveller and when one overtakes, one seeks permission first and that permission is granted in a language that both the drivers understand: no blaring of horns, just quiet signals. Driving at night is fun and even today, my son and I make a game of guessing the make of the approaching car by just looking at its headlights. Often, he is the one who guesses correctly.

Flying at night has its own charm too. The cockpit is so beautiful at night, like a bride glittering in her finest jewellery at her wedding. The dials and the lights are like diamonds and rubies, glowing in the dark. Have you seen the runway from an aeroplane at night? It is like a decorated street at a wedding function minus the blaring music, waiting for the baraat. And the groom doesn't appear on horseback or in a decorated car but arrives in a flying machine!

I've always found ways to keep myself amused and happy. Getting ready for night flying gives me a special feeling of a blind date with the stars. Also, I have the tendency to enjoy doing things which are difficult or scary for others.

Initially, take-offs and landings seem difficult, but once you get used to it, you can fly better at night. As the air settles down, there are fewer gusts of air, up draughts and down draughts that result in the bumps you feel while flying, when the Captain asks you 'please fasten your seat belts' in mid-air.

But I wanted to go beyond the limits, the airfield limits.

Every city looks beautiful at night from high up. I wanted to see how the earth, the rivers and the roads appear at night. During the day, you can see them clearly and estimate your position, but at night it's a different story altogether when they play hide-

and-seek. I loved to play the guessing games of night flying; I loved the challenge.

One incident about night flying stands out in my memory. I was still a rookie then. I progressed through the air navigation day phase but the inevitable happened in the night. I was lost, though I was so close to my destination.

It happened at the end of the triangular three-point navigation. After the navigation, the planes are asked to come over to a reporting point, which in this case was Point North —a lake seven miles north of the airfield. The planes are asked to orbit at different altitudes, the lowest one is allowed to come to the airfield and land. You must have noticed while travelling that when you look down, the airfield is there, but it takes a long time for the aircraft to land.

 I came to the reporting point and joined the orbit. It's a very boring and annoying thing to do. Ask any pilot. After a long day and especially at night, when you have only the stars above and the lights below, when there is nothing to explore and the lights down below are so misleading.

As they say, there is always light at the end of the tunnel, but that light may be that of an incoming train. There have been funny instances of pilots having mistaken the lights of roads and bridges for a runway. People have even followed lights and later found that they were the moving headlights of vehicles. Also, at times, stationary lights appear to move.

We make similar mistakes in life, we either follow the wrong targets or we are stuck in a relationship which is dead but one which we assume is moving. Life sometimes creates its own illusions and if you are not prepared, you are caught unawares.

"120, Tower," the call from the tower shook me out of my thoughts.

"Tower, 120, go ahead," I replied.

"120, you are cleared to descend and come to the airfield for landing."

"Roger, 120."

At night, when you are flying in circles for several minutes, it seems like ages, and any glimpse of light is a light of hope; one tends to make it one's destination.

The same thing happened to me. Without cross-checking the instruments, I picked what I thought were airfield lights and happily proceeded in that direction. I checked my watch and hoped the bar would be open after the gruelling day.

When I looked outside, the lights were gone. I was shocked. What had happened? Was there a power failure at the airfield or had I crossed it? I looked at the compass. It showed a steady 180°, the southerly heading to steer from Pt. North to the airfield. To check back I tried to turn, but the compass was stuck at 180°! Did that mean that I had been following the wrong direction all this while?

It was practically impossible to get lost so close to the destination, 6 nautical miles from Pt. North at a speed of 150 knots. It should have taken me not more than 2 minutes 30 seconds. I looked at the stop clock. I had not reset it.

Victor's words rang in my head, "Time is money, honey, in the air, on the ground, and everywhere. You cannot move from point A to point B without knowing how much time it will take."

And here I was, lost.

I looked down, all the lights had vanished, and when I looked up, the stars had vanished as well. I could see clouds, dark clouds. Panic was beginning to set in, I was lost… completely lost. I didn't know where I was, I didn't know how long I had been lost. I had a bad compass and now I was in the midst of thick, dark clouds and couldn't see a damn thing.

I felt it was the end of everything, all my childhood dreams seemed to fade away, how could I accept that I was as good as lost, nobody would have gotten this close to getting lost.

I remembered Victor's words: When you are lost, the first rule is 'Do not panic'. The second rule is 'Ask for help'. Just contact anybody and everybody and tell them your last known position.

And then began the battle with myself. What will people think? Here he is, this smart guy has managed to get lost, and lost so close to his destination! I swallowed my pride, my ego, my self-esteem and everything in between, and I pressed the 'talk' button.

"Tower, 120," I said, but got no response.

"Tower, this is 120," but there was still no response.

"Tower, this is 120, do you read me?" I shouted hysterically.

I tried the different channels and various frequencies but the result was the same. No response.

"So here you are, Manish, wise guy," I told myself, "All by yourself, all alone, with no one to help you." Tears rolled down my cheeks and I prayed, "God, what have I done to deserve this? God, will you guide me home?" I was desperate.

Suddenly I heard a voice in my head: "Son, come back home!"

Nobody spoke those words. I instinctively banked the aircraft at 15°, started the stop clock and calculated that if I turned with a bank of 15° I would turn 45° and in 1 minute I would turn 180°.

As I rolled out, exactly after 1 minute, the Fuel Low-Level Warning light glowed red. It indicated that I had fuel for only 15 minutes. Oddly enough, the light gave me strength in a strange way, the strength of definitiveness, whatever had to happen would happen in the next fifteen minutes, I thought.

Filled with this new strength, my mind was busy calculating. I couldn't force land the plane in darkness. If I bailed out, would the plane crash somewhere near the airfield? I shuddered when I thought of it. Even if I died, my soul would not be at peace if my actions had inadvertently hurt anyone.

The certainty of death brings a profound sense of peace, a deadly calm, and life begins to pass before your eyes as a slide show. The wonderful summer afternoons, when as kids, we were forced to take a nap and we had fun sneaking out in the garden when nobody was looking; the fights with our cousins at the dining table comparing our portions of food; the long nights spent on the rooftops waiting for the electric supply to be restored; my dad's excitement when I arrived home for a vacation; the tearful eyes of my mother every time I left home; and recently the tender love of my fiancée, the gentle touch of her fingers as she held my hand, the sweet caress…

The sad faces of my loved ones suddenly flashed past my eyes and shook me. I said to myself: "You cannot die, Manish. Not today, not ever."

"Tower, this is 120, can you hear me?"

"120, Tower, report position." Was the voice in my ears real or was I dreaming, hallucinating?

I screamed, "120 is lost!"

This time, Victor's voice came on, "Manish, don't panic, just relax."

"I'm not panicking, Sir; I'm lost, and feeling desperate. I really need help, Sir. My compass has failed. I don't know where I am, I don't know where I am headed. I have limited fuel. Please help me, Sir!" I divulged it all in a single breath.

"Manish, we have you on radar, son." Victor's voice was deliberate and calm. I felt reassured when I heard him speak. "You are quite close. If you follow exactly what I say, we will get you home, son. Are you ready to follow my instructions?"

Nothing is more comforting than knowing that you are in safe hands. I knew I could blindly follow Victor's instructions to the last word, the last syllable.

Chapter Thirteen

IN HIM I TRUST

I was more than eager to follow Victor's instructions. After a few turns and losing some height, I emerged from the clouds. Very soon, he positioned me in line with the runway lights.

"Can you see the runway, Manish?"

"Yes, Sir!" I said joyously.

"Welcome home, son, you are cleared to land."

"Thank you, Sir!" My voice choked as tears of gratitude almost blurred my vision.

As my tyres kissed the earth, I felt relieved, rested and protected, like a child returning to the security of his mother's embrace after an especially traumatic experience.

I had arrived! It was a glorious feeling. Everything looked more beautiful, even the grass looked greener beneath the dim red wing-tip lights. I wondered if astronauts felt the same when they returned. It was wonderful to be alive.

"Manish, do you want to switch off on the taxi track?"

"I have fuel left, Sir, I can go to the dispersal."

Victor signed off. "Ok, going off, will see you soon. PS or RK?" he asked, referring to the popular brands of whiskey at that time.

As I switched off, it began to rain. I saw a man coming towards me with an umbrella. He tilted it up and looked at me, it was Victor. With tears in his eyes, he said, "We thought we had lost you."

"No, Sir, with you around I can never be lost," I replied, equally moved.

I jumped out of the cockpit and he hugged me like a long-lost friend. He took out a packet of Camel, my brand of cigarettes, and handed it to me. I was touched that he, a non-smoker, was carrying it.

"Don't be surprised, son. Today I will smoke with you."

Others were waiting for us in the briefing room. The CI handed me a glass of whisky and toasted: "Happy Birthday! Three Cheers to Manish!"

"Hip, hip, hurray!"

"Cheers!"

A big gulp of the drink helped me calm my nerves and I narrated the entire episode. I was told that the weather had suddenly deteriorated. Lots of stories were exchanged and lots of lessons were learnt on getting lost. Contrary to my fear of ridicule, I was praised for shouting aloud those three words that one hates to admit: "I am lost."

I wondered if it was my intuition that had made me turn back and head to safety.

Chapter Fourteen

FLYING IN FORMATION

It is delightful to have someone by your side, someone to lead or someone to follow, especially in the air. The sight of another plane so close to you, very few have the privilege to witness it. But with the privilege comes the responsibility. Being cleared for Formation Flying determines that one can take responsibility. The pilot is adept at handling himself; he makes limited errors himself and can compensate for the errors of others.

The briefing for the Formation Flying phase was extensive. It began with how to catch up with a Leader, closing in, and the responsibilities of a Leader. Learning something new has always been exciting and fun for me and I looked forward to it.

The Radio Telephony checks in Formation Flying are odd.

Only the Leader calls the tower. The follower called the No 2 only acknowledges the call. If the formation call sign is TIGER, it will be:

Leader: "Tiger, RT."

No 2: "Tiger 2."

Leader: "Reading you, strength 5, break, break, Tiger Two aircraft formation, start!"

Tower: "Tiger, start-up approved."

One of my friends was not attentive during the briefing. He and his Instructor were scheduled to fly as Leader. He was shocked when his instructor found that they were alone at line-up. All the while, my friend thought he was No. 2 and acknowledged the calls. We had a great laugh at it, no doubt, but it's true that one can learn so much from others' mistakes.

So, I was all strapped up in the aircraft when the RT calls began.

"Maverick RT."

"Maverick 2."

We were No. 2. It feels so good when you know you will have company in the air.

In the earlier stages, you cannot do a take-off with the Leader. You have to catch the one who is already up in the air. As per the procedure, the Leader, after take-off, makes a circuit and flies over the runway; you must time your take-off in such a way that you are airborne, keeping the Leader in sight, and then close in. Victor showed me all this.

It's very exciting. You are prepared, ready for take-off, waiting for the Leader, anticipating his call.

"Maverick, roll!"

"Rolling now."

Then with all your expertise, you adjust your power and speed to close in. If you are slow, the gap between you and your Leader increases, to the extent that you will not be able to catch up. The Leader won't slow down for you. **Leaders are not supposed to slow down.**

Don continued, "You must be ready for the Leader. He will make one pass over the runway and you have to catch him. You have to be careful; if you aren't, you will be following someone else who may not be the Leader. So, keep your eyes on the horizon looking for your Leader.

We waited eagerly on the runway after giving the call.

"Maverick 2, ready."

"Maverick 2, roll now."

"Maverick 2, rolling now."

And there he was above us. Victor executed a perfect take-off. I had my eyes glued on the Leader's plane. It dazzled beautifully in the morning sun. As the leader turned ahead of us, I noticed Victor turning with him but pointing the plane ahead of the Leader's.

"Won't we get ahead of him this way?"

"This is called the 'angle of lead.' If you head behind him, you'll be never able to catch him. You should be ahead of the Leader to catch him. This is the technique to close in to a Leader," he explained.

That was true. Slowly, the distance between us began to lessen and within seconds we were so close that I could hear the sound of his propellers. Victor was continuously making finer corrections with speed and power.

"Maverick 2, in position," he gave the call.

We were line astern, behind the Leader. I had never seen another aircraft so close. It felt like an extension of ours.

"Roger. We begin now."

Victor continued to explain, "You know, it takes a lot of effort to be a good follower. When you are alone, you must be mentally ahead of your aircraft. In formation, you must be mentally ahead of the Leader and anticipate his moves.

I could see that. As the exercise began, Don was following him meticulously. He turned the instant the Leader turned and rolled out of the turn precisely in position. For someone watching from the ground, it would seem as if both planes were being flown by a single pilot. This was the beauty of flying in formation when the parts seemed to become a whole.

He continued, "Flying in formation is all about trust. You must have faith in the ability of your Leader. The Leader has to prove it by example. He can neither make sudden changes nor do anything unpredictable. Likewise, the Leader has to have faith in his followers. Just as you love to fly with an able Leader, the Leader will also look for a capable No. 2, capable of being led."

I nodded.

"You have the controls, Manish, follow him."

"I have the controls," I said and took over. I realized that I had to have all the skills at my command to prove to Victor that I was a worthy follower because soon it would be him I would have to follow. In my enthusiasm, I was making abrupt changes.

"Don't be tense, Manish," said Victor. "Follow the sequence of Change-Check-Hold-Adjust. Whenever you make any changes, check for the effect, hold for some time for the desired effect to take place, and then make the finer adjustments. If you keep making abrupt changes, you will get out of the rhythm."

I had heard of it; it is a state when you are out of sync. When you try to move forward, you fall back and when you want to stop, the inertia keeps you moving forward.

Even life has its own rhythm and only a few of us follow it. Sometimes we try to move so fast that we cannot stop even if we want to. It is the hectic pace of life or some destructive habit we want to change but cannot. At other times, we move so slowly and lag so far behind that life seems to pass us by. We become meek spectators instead of being active participants.

My philosophical ruminations were interrupted by the Leader's call, "Maverick, line abreast."

This is a position alongside the leader, at an angle, only slightly behind. When the Leader finds that you are comfortable following him, he invites you by his side to this position of honour. As we got into the position, at a distance of one wing tip apart, I found the Leader welcoming us with a broad smile. Getting into the line-abreast position is a dangerous move. While the Leader maintains his position, the No. 2 comes near him in stages. Coming very fast can unnerve the Leader and even throw him off position.

When a Guru sits in meditation, the pupil comes slowly and silently takes his seat next to him.

The other aircraft was so close that I could almost touch it.

"Will you be able to maintain it here?" Victor asked as we got into the position.

I wasn't prepared for it but Victor handed me the controls anyway. As soon as I took over the controls, I started creeping in, crossing the safe limit between us, and invading the Leader's space.

"Slow down," Victor almost shouted.

I tried, but the damage was done, and the Leader broke off.

Victor sighed in anguish, "You cannot move so fast, Manish. As soon as someone gives you the right to come close, you have to maintain the specified separation, moving fast scares the other person."

He was right. I was so absorbed that I thought I was drifting apart. I could have easily maintained the distance. I was so scared of losing him that I actually lost him! Luckily, it was just an evasive manoeuvre by the Leader. He was again flying steady.

"Call in position," instructed the Leader.

Victor said, "This time, Manish, get into position yourself."

I was slowly trying to get into position from the right when Victor shouted, "Watch out for the bird!"

The Leader had suddenly turned towards us. Before I realised it, Victor had taken over the controls, he broke off to the right, shouting, "I have the controls!"

While I was concentrating on the Leader closing in and while the Leader was watching me, an eagle headed straight towards him. Victor was the first to spot it. The eagle was approaching from the Leader's left and to avoid hitting it, he quickly turned right.

"When you are in formation, not only do you have to ensure the safety of the other, warning him of the imminent danger, but you also must anticipate his moves and mistakes. It is also possible that suddenly you have to take the lead. Even when you are No. 2. Think as a Leader and always be prepared to take the lead," said Victor, settling the plane.

Until then, the Leader had positioned himself on our wings and was following us.

He called, "Sorry for that, I'm following you now."

Victor continued, "You cannot be a worthy Leader if you are not a good follower."

After a few more sorties as No. 2, I was cleared to go solo, all alone, flying with a Leader. It was time for me to show my leadership skills.

Chapter Fifteen

BECOMING A LEADER

Being a Leader is a huge responsibility. You are responsible for the lives of others. The effect of your actions and inactions are not limited to yourself. It affects all those who follow you as well. It makes you feel powerful, but along with power comes responsibility. When you are flying as a Leader on your call sign, pride echoes in your voice. Your voice commands respect, even the wind seems to stop to listen to a Leader.

With Victor, I made the pass over the runway looking out for my No.2.

"Maverick, call ready."

No response.

"Maverick, do you hear me?"

Victor sniffed the impatience in my voice. "Manish, as a Leader, you cannot be impatient. You must give your No. 2 the lead time."

"Maverick 2, ready to roll." My No. 2 responded.

"Maverick 2 roll now."

It was a pleasure seeing my No. 2 begin to roll down the runway, and I felt like a father watching his toddler take the first baby steps in life. As I flew over him, I lost him visually. All I had to do now was to fly as precisely as possible and wait for his call.

"Maverick in position," he called.

The moment I got the call I knew I had four lives in my hands and had to be more cautious and deliberate with my actions. The burden of responsibility is great but so is the pride, the pleasure and the satisfaction. I flew with precision, maintaining height, speed and direction accurately. It was not only my professional competence at stake but also the faith of my instructor, who had cleared me to be the Leader. I glanced at Victor and saw him filled with pride. There is no better satisfaction than seeing your pupil, your prodigy, take over the leadership role. Very soon, I would have that satisfaction too.

Chapter Sixteen

YOU HAVE THE CONTROLS

It took twelve years to make it happen. I was posted as an instructor after my Flight Instructor's course, eagerly waiting for my first pupil. Teaching, instructing, leading, mentoring, coaching —all this is an urge. It is like any other biological need such as hunger, thirst or sleep.

As soon as you learn something, the only way to perfect the knowledge or the skill is to teach it to others. The more one does that, the more one grows in conviction and depth on the subject.

When the pupil is ready, the Master appears and alternately when the Master is ready, the pupil appears.

It was Arnab, a bright-eyed, medium-built Flight Cadet who greeted me in the hallway. "Good morning, Sir. I have been assigned to you. You are my instructor, Sir."

A thrill of happiness went up my spine. I could not hide my smile. Being the youngest instructor had its own excitement. At the Flight Instructor's school, they prepare you to become a Flight Instructor but no one prepares you for this moment when you have a rookie looking up to you, smiling at you with all his confidence, his gaze saying, "Will you teach me all that you know?"

I think that is the difference between a Leader and a Guru. The Leader leads by example, he teaches "What to" but a Guru teaches "How to".

Will he be as keen to be a pilot as I was, I wondered. Arnab almost guessed what was going on in my mind.

"Sir, you know, I had a government scholarship in a flying club for Civil Aviation, but I wanted to train with the best in order to be the best."

The pride on his face and the determination in his voice was more than enough to quell my doubts.

"Ok, Arnab, I'll teach you all that I know and if you put in your best, I'm sure you will be the best. We'll begin tomorrow."

The young man tried to match his steps with mine as we walked towards our plane. It looked golden in the morning sunlight, like the golden chariot of Mahabharata, with Krishna and Arjuna all ready to conquer the sky. I remembered Victor and Mitra and their lessons about life. More than flying, they had helped me become a man, a man of integrity and purpose. Today, I had the torch in my hand, to light the spark in another soul, to begin teaching all that I had been taught, and much more.

I did not want Arnab to make the same mistakes that I had made in flying and in life. So, as we lined up on the runway, I told him, "Pick-up a point on the runway to maintain direction," assisting him in the take-off. I could see the excitement on his face and the satisfaction of making it here. I remembered my first take-off with Victor over 12 years ago and smiled, he smiled back knowingly. He knew I was happy to have him there with me.

After settling down in the exercise area, I told Arnab, "You have the controls." As he took over, I realized the relief I felt in laying down the burden of faith on someone, trusting someone with my life, someone who I barely knew.

"I have the controls" he responded and took over.

There is something magical in these four words. With these words, I have seen ordinary people turn into extraordinary beings, connected with the supreme power within, the grit and determination on their faces, shoulders squared to take full responsibility, the authority in their voice, nothing less than becoming Gods and Masters of their destiny.

"You have the controls."

"Yes, Sir, I have the controls."